LIFE SKILLS
IN THE PACIFIC

Basic Cooking

Sisilia Tawali

OXFORD

Contents

Cooking in Papua New Guinea 2
How to select and prepare food for cooking 4
Types of stoves in Papua New Guinea 6
Basic recipes 7
aibika 8
aupa 10
banana 14
beans 18
bread 20
breadfruit 23
cakes 24
cassava 26
chicken 28
coconut 31
eggplant. 32
fish 34
peanuts 41
potato. 44
sago 47
scones. 50
sweet potato 52
taro 54
tea time varieties. 56
yams 60
Glossary. 62

Introduction

Everyone can cook creative meals using basic ingredients that are cheap and readily available. Delicious meals can be produced by combining staple foods such as sweet potato, banana and sago with onion, ginger or garlic. This book contains a wide variety of recipes for simple and tasty meals that you can cook easily at home or school.

This book complements the newly introduced 'Making a Living' subject for upper primary students. It supports the philosophy of Education, which emphasises relevant education and self-reliance. It teaches students useful skills and relevant knowledge to enable them to become useful members of their local communities.

Strand: *Better Living*
Sub Strand: *Healthy Living*
Outcomes: 7.2.1: *Identify aspects of a nutritious diet and suggest how and where they might obtain, preserve, process and prepare these foods to meet nutritional requirements*
8.2.1: *Investigate and implement practical ways to produce and prepare food for personal consumption or to generate an income*

I encourage everyone to try out these recipes. They use basic ingredients that everyone has at home, the steps are easy to follow, and the meals are delicious to eat.

Happy cooking and eating!

Sisilia Tawali

Cooking in Papua New Guinea

People in different provinces of Papua New Guinea use different methods of cooking. Often food is cooked on open fires or hot coals, especially in provincial areas. Most foods are cooked in coconut cream or boiling water.

The most common methods of cooking foods in Papua New Guinea are listed below.

Traditional cooking methods

Mumu

Mumuing is a popular method of cooking in Papua New Guinea. There are many traditional ways of cooking a mumu.

Special mumu stones are heated until they are very hot and then placed in a shallow hole in the ground. Foods such as root crops, vegetables, meat and chicken are cleaned and washed, then wrapped in banana leaves to form a big parcel. (Coconut cream can be added to the food at this stage.) This parcel is placed on the hot stones and covered with more banana leaves so that the steam doesn't escape from the food as it cooks.

The food cooks in several hours, depending on the size of the parcel. The banana leaves and coconut cream give a special flavour to the food.

Igir

Igir is another interesting way to cook food. This method is mainly used by people living on the coast.

The food is cooked in coconut cream in a big flat-bottomed pot. The coconut cream is obtained by scraping coconuts, adding water and squeezing out the cream. A person cooking for a family of four would need to use five coconuts to get enough cream.

Stones are heated until they are very hot, then dipped in cold water for a few seconds to remove any ashes. They are then placed into the pot with the coconut cream. As with a mumu, food is wrapped in banana leaves to form parcels. These parcels of food are placed into the coconut cream and the pot is covered. The food is cooked in a very short time.

Other cooking methods

Steaming

The food is cooked in the steam from boiling liquid so that the food does not touch the liquid. This is a very healthy way to cook food.

Boiling

The food is cooked in boiling water. You should never throw away water that has been used to boil vegetables, as it contains vitamins and minerals that have been dissolved from the food. You can use this water to make soup.

Stewing

The food is cooked in a small amount of water or other liquid with the juices of the food itself, which are very nutritious. The liquid becomes a tasty sauce for the food.

Grilling

There are four methods of grilling:

- grilling in the fire, where the food is put directly onto the hot coals of the fire. It is best to grill food on or over the fire to prevent the food from burning.
- grilling on a stick over a fire. This is the best way to grill small pieces of food.
- grilling on a wire rack over hot coals.
- using the grill on an electric or gas stove.

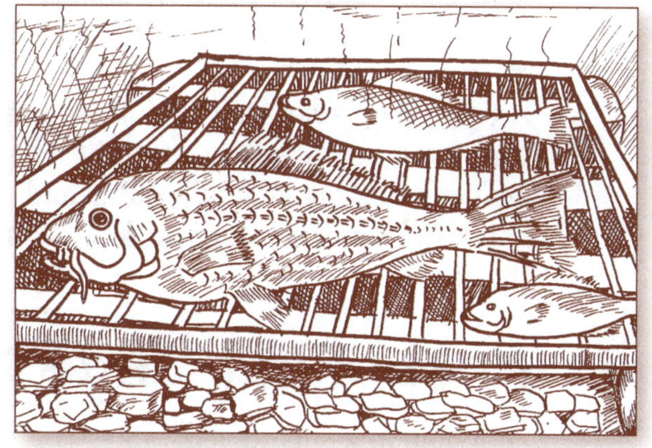

Frying

The food is cooked in fat or oil in a pan on top of a fire. The fat should be heated in the pan before adding the food, but care should be taken as the food will burn if the fat is too hot.

Baking

The food is cooked in an 'oven' using dry heat. Food can be baked in tins and saucepans over a fire, ground ovens, drum ovens, or electric and gas ovens.

Roasting

The food is cooked in an oven with fat or oil.

How to select and prepare food for cooking

Your meals will taste better if you cook with good quality ingredients. It is important to select vegetables and other foods carefully and to store them properly so that they stay fresh. Some foods need special preparation before they can be used in cooking.

Selecting and storing vegetables

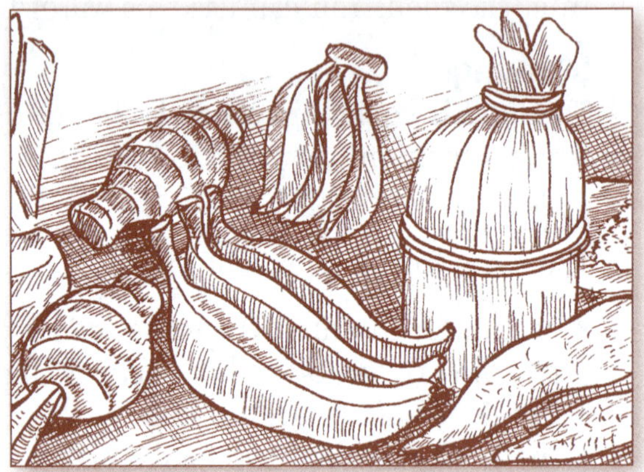

If buying vegetables at the market, always check them carefully before buying. Many vegetables are sold in bundles, so it is important to check all parts of the vegetables. The leaves may look very fresh but the middle part of the vegetable may be full of insects or starting to rot.

Store vegetables in a cool, dry, well-ventilated place. Strong sunlight and heat can destroy many vitamins and minerals in food so we must keep it in the shade.

Preparing vegetables for cooking

Chopping and slicing vegetables is a skill that everyone can obtain with practice. If vegetables are not sliced, ensure the vegetable pieces are all of a similar size so that they will cook evenly. Most leaf vegetables in Papua New Guinea are cooked whole without needing to be chopped or cut.

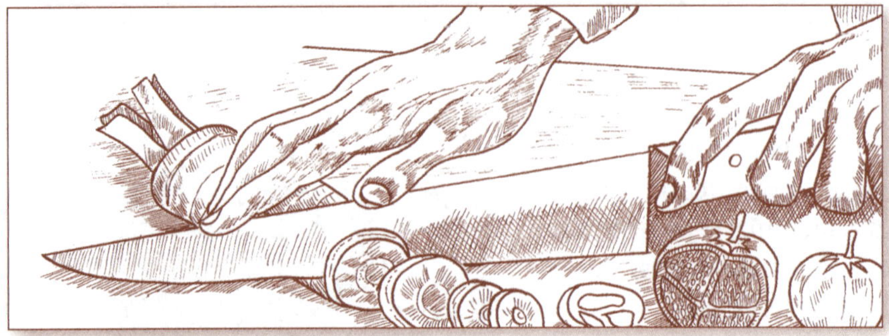

If several different types of vegetables are being used for a recipe, those that need a longer cooking time should be added to your cooking first so that all the vegetables are ready at the same time.

Important cooking information

- Make sure you always wash vegetables before cooking them, but do not soak them in water as this will take the nutrients out of the vegetables.
- Cook vegetables for as short a time as possible. If the food is cooked for too long the vitamins and minerals will be lost.

Useful hints

- Always cut eggplant in the water to avoid discolouring.

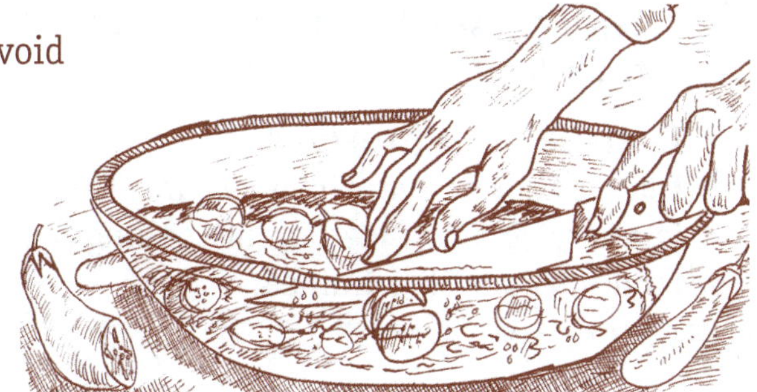

- Keep a round stone in the kitchen to crush garlic, ginger and so on.

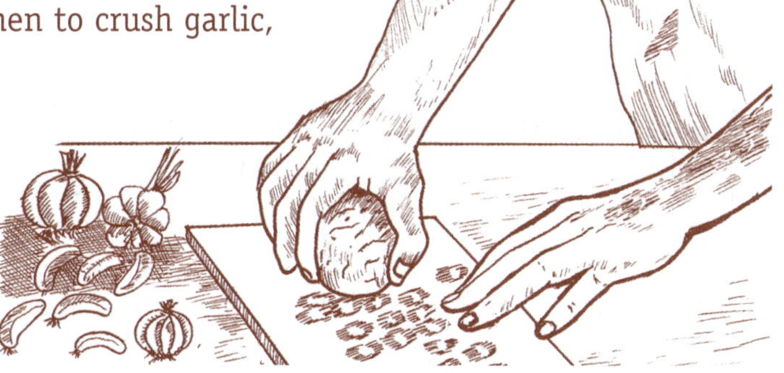

- To stop coconut cream from curdling while cooking, stir it every now and then.

- Yams are sticky when you peel them. It is best to wash and dry the yams before peeling, then slice and cook them.
- You can add flavour to your meals by frying onion, ginger and garlic before adding the other ingredients.

Types of stoves in Papua New Guinea

As living expenses in Papua New Guinea are very high, many families struggle to find the cheapest way of living. This includes finding a cheaper way of cooking food.

Families use different types of stoves for cooking. Some common stoves are listed below.

Charcoal and firewood

Food is cooked over the open fire. This is a very common method of cooking food in Papua New Guinea.

Sawdust stoves

These stoves are a cheap method of cooking food. They need less firewood as they use mainly sawdust, which can be obtained from sawmills free of charge.

Gas and electric stoves

The easiest way to cook food is by using a gas or electric stove. However, gas and electricity are expensive and therefore many families cannot afford to use these stoves.

Kerosene primus stoves

These stoves are very common. They are used by many families as a cheaper alternative to gas and electricity.

Basic recipes

The recipes in this book are simple to make and use basic ingredients that are easy to find. The recipes are also nutritious as they contain all the different types of food that the body needs to stay healthy:

Energy foods (carbohydrates)

These foods give us energy quickly to work and play. Some energy foods are sweet potato, banana, cassava, taro, coconut and sago.

Body-building foods (proteins)

These foods help our bodies to grow and remain healthy. Some body-building foods are beans, peanuts, yams, meat, fish and eggs.

Protective foods (vitamins and minerals)

These foods keep us healthy and make our bodies work properly. Some protective foods are green leaves such as aibika and aupa, vegetables and fruits.

Fats and oils

These are stored in our bodies to give us energy over a longer period of time and keep us warm. Some fats and oils are oil, butter and margarine.

Adding flavour to food

Spices and herbs add flavour to cooking. The cheapest flavourings used in cooking are ***onion***, ***ginger*** and ***garlic***. Delicious meals can be cooked just by using these three ingredients to add flavour.

Many spices, herbs and plants grow wild around Papua New Guinea, but not all people know how to use them for cooking. Ask someone who knows about the herbs and plants growing in your area to teach you how to harvest them and use them in cooking.

A wide variety of spices is available in Papua New Guinea, but these are very expensive if you buy them from the supermarket.

Aibika

Aibika contains a large amount of protein and is a very nutritious food. The young leaves are cooked in coconut cream or water. They can also be fried.

Aibika comes in a great number of varieties. It is grown in most parts of Papua New Guinea. This crop grows well in good, well-composted soils.

Aibika with potatoes

INGREDIENTS

3–4 bundles of aibika	4 medium-sized potatoes
1 small onion	1 piece of ginger
a few cloves of garlic	chilli (optional)
oil for frying	salt to taste

PROCEDURE

1. Clean and wash the aibika. Put it in the sun to dry the leaves.
2. Chop the aibika finely.
3. Peel the potatoes and slice them thinly.
4. Slice the onion and crush the ginger, garlic and chilli (if using).
5. Heat the oil in a saucepan. When it is hot, add the onion, ginger and garlic and fry until they turn light brown. Add the potatoes and stir well.
6. Lower the heat and cook the potatoes until they are almost tender.
7. Add the aibika and stir until well mixed. Add salt to taste.
8. Cook on a low heat until the aibika is well cooked and the potatoes are tender.

Note: *This recipe is very nice with roti or puri.*

Aibika with beans and carrots

INGREDIENTS

3 bundles of aibika

a handful of string beans

1 piece of ginger

oil for frying

3 medium-sized carrots

1 small onion

5 cloves of garlic

salt to taste

PROCEDURE

1 Clean and wash the aibika. Put it in the sun to dry the leaves.

2 Chop the aibika finely.

3 Chop the carrots and beans into small pieces.

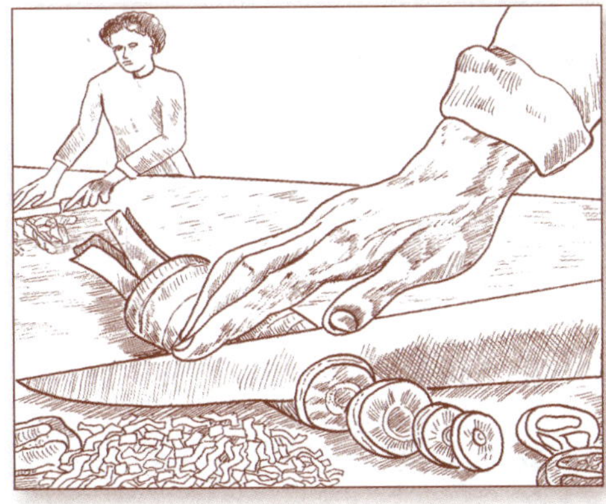

4 Chop the onion and crush the ginger and garlic.

5 Heat the oil in a saucepan and fry the onion, ginger and garlic until golden brown.

6 Add the chopped carrots and beans and stir for a few minutes.

7 Cover the saucepan and cook for about 6 minutes until the vegetables are almost tender.

8 Lower the heat and add the aibika. Stir well and cook until the aibika is well cooked.

9 Add salt to taste and mix well.

 **Note**: *This recipe is very nice with roti or puri.*

Aupa

Aupa contains a large amount of protein and is a very nutritious food to include in your family's diet. It should be cooked and can be eaten hot or cold. When cooking aupa, use the softer stems as well as the leaves.

This small plant grows easily from seed in almost any kind of soil, provided it gets plenty of water. It prefers wet weather and so should be planted at the beginning of the wet season. Aupa can be damaged by grubs chewing the leaves of the young plant. It is not affected by disease.

Aupa with tomatoes

INGREDIENTS

3 bundles of aupa

1 small onion

5 cloves of garlic

3 medium-sized tomatoes

oil for frying

salt to taste

PROCEDURE

1. Clean and wash the aupa. Drain the water well after washing. Chop the aupa and put it aside.
2. Chop the onion and crush the garlic.
3. Chop the tomatoes.
4. Heat the oil in a saucepan and add the onion and garlic. Fry until golden brown.
5. Add the aupa and salt to taste. Fry for 3 minutes.
6. Add the tomatoes and cook for a further few minutes. Do not overcook.

Aupa with potatoes

INGREDIENTS

3 bundles of aupa

3–4 medium-sized potatoes

1 small onion

5 cloves of garlic

1 piece of ginger

1 chilli (optional)

2 tablespoons of oil

salt to taste

PROCEDURE

1. Clean and wash the aupa. Drain the aupa and chop the leaves.
2. Peel the potatoes. Slice them thinly or cut them into thin squares.
3. Slice the onion and crush the garlic, ginger and chilli (if using).
4. Heat the oil in a saucepan and add the onion, garlic and ginger. Fry until golden brown.
5. Add the potatoes and cook over a gentle heat. Stir every now and then until the potatoes are almost tender.
6. Add the chopped aupa and cook for a few more minutes.
7. When cooked, add salt to taste.

Aupa fritters

INGREDIENTS

1 bundle of aupa
5 cloves of garlic
chopped herbs (optional)
salt to taste
1 medium-sized onion
1 chilli
1½ cups of self-raising flour
oil for frying

PROCEDURE

1 Wash the aupa and chop the leaves very finely.
2 Finely chop the onion and add to the aupa.
3 Crush the garlic and chilli and add to the aupa. Add the herbs (if using).
4 Add the flour to the aupa, then add salt and just enough water to make a thick batter.
5 Heat the oil in a frying pan. When hot, drop spoonfuls of the batter into the oil.

6 Fry until golden brown. Drain well before serving.

 **Note:** *These fritters can be eaten hot or cold.*

Aupa fritters with potatoes, carrots and chokos

INGREDIENTS

1–2 bundles of aupa

1 large carrot

1 medium-sized onion

1 chilli (optional)

oil for frying

1 medium-sized potato

1 medium-sized choko

4–5 cloves of garlic

2 cups of self-raising flour

PROCEDURE

1. Wash the aupa and chop the leaves very finely.
2. Peel and coarsely grate the potato.
3. Mix the grated potato with the chopped aupa.
4. Wash, peel and grate the carrot and choko. Add to the potato and aupa.
5. Chop the onion and crush the garlic and chilli (if using). Add to the aupa mixture.
6. Add the flour to the aupa mixture, then add enough water to make a thick batter.
7. Mix well and put aside for 10 minutes.
8. Heat the oil in a frying pan and drop spoonfuls of the mixture into the oil. If the mixture doesn't hold together, just add a little more flour.
9. Fry until golden brown. Drain well before serving.

Note: *This recipe is very nice with tomato sauce.*
If using plain flour, add 2 teaspoons of baking powder to 2 cups of plain flour.

Banana

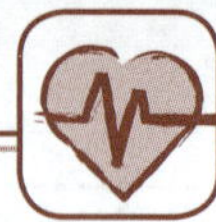

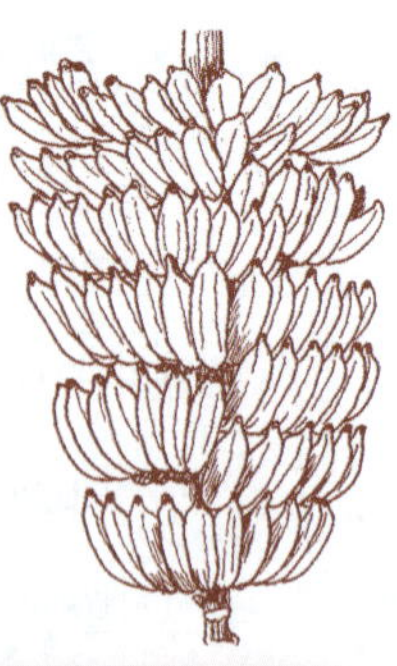

Bananas are a high-energy food. They can be grown in a wide variety of soils provided there is good drainage and adequate fertility and moisture. Bananas do not grow well in very sandy or hard soils.

Bananas do not store well, so they should be harvested only when they are required for cooking. If bananas are harvested too early they will not taste good.

Banana curry

INGREDIENTS

5 green cooking bananas

1 cup of water

3 tablespoons of oil

crushed garlic and ginger

salt to taste

crushed chilli (optional)

1 teaspoon of curry powder

PROCEDURE

1. Peel the bananas. Cut into little squares and place in the water.
2. Heat the oil in a pan and fry the crushed garlic and ginger.
3. Drain the bananas and add to the garlic and ginger. Cook for a few minutes.
4. Stir the salt, chilli (if using) and curry powder into the banana mixture and cook for a few minutes over a low heat. If the bananas start to stick to the bottom of the pan, sprinkle some water into the pan.
5. Cook until the bananas are tender.

Note: *Serve hot or cold.*
This recipe is very nice with roti.

Bananas and sago

INGREDIENTS

2 cups of sago

1 banana leaf

8 cups of water

¾ cup of ripe mashed banana

2 coconuts

PROCEDURE

1. Put the sago in a dish and rub between your fingers to break up any lumps.
2. Add the mashed banana and mix well. Put aside.
3. Heat the banana leaf over the fire and cut into pieces about 25 cm (10 inches) long and 20 cm (8 inches) wide.
4. Put a tablespoon of sago mixture on a piece of leaf, flatten the mixture, and fold the leaf to make it look like a parcel. Tie it with a piece of string. Repeat until all the mixture has been used.
5. Boil about 5 cups of water and drop the parcels in the boiling water. Cook until the sago turns brown.
6. Remove the sago parcels from the boiling water. Unwrap the leaves and place the sago parcels in a dish.
7. Scrape the coconuts and add 3 cups of water. Squeeze the thick coconut milk out.
8. Heat the coconut milk on a low heat until cream forms on top. Do not let it boil.
9. Scoop the cream off the top and pour it over the sago parcels. Turn the parcels around so that the cream covers the sago well.

Note: *This dish is delicious when eaten with fish. Cook other vegetables in any leftover coconut cream.*

Banana pikelets

INGREDIENTS

1 egg
1 mashed banana
1 teaspoon of baking powder
1 teaspoon of baking soda
1 tablespoon of melted butter
½ cup of sugar
1½ cups of plain flour
¼ teaspoon of salt
¾ cup of milk
extra butter for frying

PROCEDURE

1 Beat the egg and sugar together.
2 Add the mashed banana and mix until combined.
3 Sift the flour, baking powder and salt and add to the banana mixture.
4 Dissolve the baking soda in the milk and add to the mixture.
5 Mix the batter well, then add the melted butter. Stir gently.
6 Heat the extra butter in a frying pan.
7 Drop dessertspoons of the mixture into the pan. Wait until bubbles have formed on the tops of the pikelets, then turn over and cook on the other side until golden brown.

Note: *These pikelets can be eaten hot or cold.*

Banana scones

INGREDIENTS

2 cups of plain flour

¼ teaspoon of salt

3 teaspoons of baking powder

½ cup of sugar

½ cup of mashed banana

2 tablespoons of melted butter

1 egg

2 tablespoons of milk

PROCEDURE

1. Sift the flour, salt, baking powder and sugar together. Put aside.
2. Beat the banana, melted butter, egg and milk together.
3. Pour this mixture into the flour mixture and mix gently until well mixed.
4. Grease a baking sheet and place spoonfuls of mixture on the sheet.
5. Bake in a moderate oven until the scones are golden brown.

Beans

Beans are a very nutritious food as they are rich in protein and help the body to grow. Many different kinds of beans grow in Papua New Guinea.

Beans are easy to grow. The seeds should be planted in soil that has been well dug. If the plant is a climbing plant, it should be tied to a stick staked in the ground to help it grow.

Beans with potatoes, eggplant and coconut cream

INGREDIENTS

2 cups of beans
3 medium-sized potatoes
3–4 eggplants
1 clove of garlic
1 piece of ginger
oil for frying
2 teaspoons of curry powder
salt to taste
1 coconut

PROCEDURE

1. Wash the beans and cut into pieces roughly 5 cm (2 inches) long.
2. Peel and wash the potatoes and cut into quarters.
3. Wash and chop the eggplants.
4. Crush the garlic and ginger.
5. Heat the oil in a saucepan. Add the crushed ginger and garlic and fry for a few minutes.
6. Add the beans, potatoes and eggplants.
7. Scrape the coconut and squeeze out the coconut cream.
8. When the vegetables are almost cooked, add the coconut cream and stir well. Cook for a few more minutes until the vegetables are cooked.

Note: *For variety, you can use a chicken cube instead of curry powder.*

Beans with tomatoes

INGREDIENTS

3 cups of cut beans

2 medium tomatoes

3–4 cloves of garlic

1 piece of ginger

3 tablespoons of oil

1½ teaspoons of curry powder

salt to taste

PROCEDURE

1. Wash the beans and cut into small pieces.
2. Chop the tomatoes.
3. Crush the garlic and ginger.
4. Heat the oil in a saucepan. Add the crushed ginger and garlic and cook until light brown.
5. Add the beans and curry powder. Cover the saucepan with a lid and cook for 5 minutes on a low heat.
6. Add the tomatoes, stir well and cook with the lid on for a further 5–6 minutes or until cooked. Add salt to taste.

Snake beans with coconut

INGREDIENTS

3 spring onions

3 cups of beans

3 tablespoons of oil

1 cup of grated coconut

salt to taste

½ cup of water

crushed garlic and ginger (optional)

PROCEDURE

1. Wash the spring onions and beans and chop into small pieces.
2. Heat the oil in a saucepan.
3. Add the grated coconut and fry for 5 minutes.
4. Add the onion and beans.
5. Add salt to taste and cook on a low heat.
6. Sprinkle the water over the beans. Cover the saucepan with a lid and cook on low heat for another 6–7 minutes or until cooked. Serve hot or cold.

Note: *Crushed ginger and garlic can be added when frying the coconut.*
This recipe goes very nicely with Indian bread.

Bread

Bread is a useful source of energy. Although many varieties of bread can be bought at the stores, it is much cheaper to make your own fresh bread. Bread can be eaten as a supplement with many of the recipes in this book.

White bread

INGREDIENTS

½ cup of oil or butter

2½ teaspoons of salt

2 tablespoons of dry yeast

½ cup of sugar

3½ cups of hot water

9½ cups of plain flour

PROCEDURE

1. Put the oil or butter, sugar and salt in a dish with 3½ cups of hot water. Stir until the butter melts (if using butter).
2. Let the mixture cool until it is lukewarm, then stir in the yeast.
3. Let the mixture stand for 5 minutes.
4. Add 4 cups of flour and mix well.
5. Add the rest of the flour and knead until the dough is smooth.
6. Put the dough in a greased bowl for an hour until it rises.
7. Punch down the dough and form into loaves.
8. Put the loaves in greased pans and allow the dough to rise for an hour or so.
9. Bake for around 45 minutes or until golden brown.

Puris (Indian fried bread)

INGREDIENTS

3 cups of plain wholemeal flour

about 1½ cups of warm water

1 teaspoon of salt

oil for deep frying

PROCEDURE

1. Sift the flour into a large mixing bowl and add the salt.
2. Slowly add the warm water and knead for a few minutes until the mixture forms a stiff dough.
3. Take a small piece of dough and form a ball. Sprinkle with some dry flour and roll out the ball of dough until it is fairly thin.

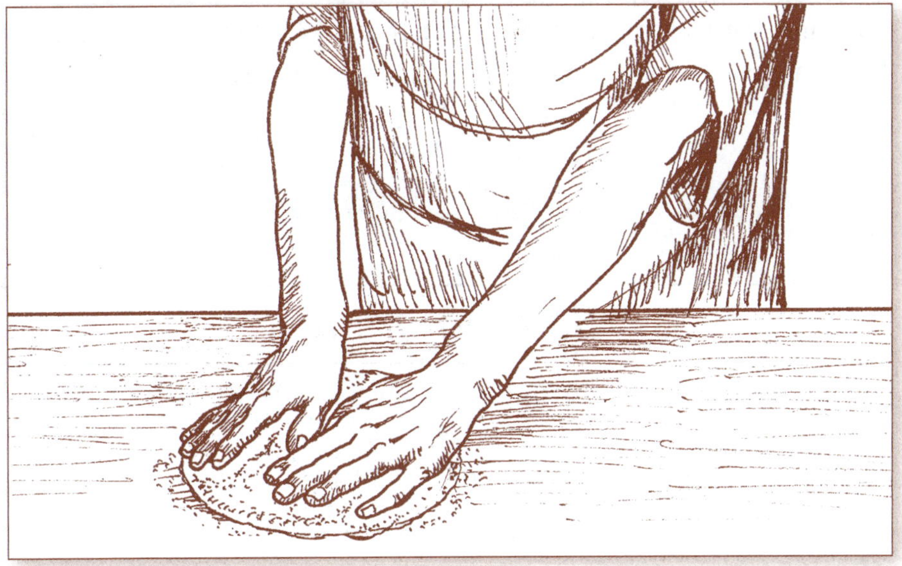

4. Repeat this process until all the puris have been rolled out. Make sure they don't touch each other as they will stick together.
5. Line up all the puris on a clean tea towel.
6. Heat the oil in a frying pan and fry the puris quickly on each side until golden brown.
7. Drain well before serving.

 **Note:** *Puris can be eaten hot or cold with any Indian dish.*

Indian bread (chapatis or roti)

INGREDIENTS

3 cups of plain wholemeal flour

1 teaspoon of salt

1 cup of water

PROCEDURE

1. Mix together 2½ cups of flour and the salt.
2. Add the water and mix to a firm dough.
3. Knead the dough for 10 minutes, then put it aside for 15 minutes.
4. Shape the dough into small balls and coat with the remaining flour.
5. Roll out each ball into a circle about 10 cm (4 inches) in diameter.
6. Fry in a lightly oiled frying pan for about 2 minutes on each side.

Banana bread

INGREDIENTS

1 cup of butter or margarine

3 eggs

4 cups of self-raising flour

1½ cups of sugar

5 mashed bananas

1 cup of crushed roasted peanuts

PROCEDURE

1. Cream the butter and sugar until very smooth.
2. Beat the eggs and fold into the butter and sugar mixture.
3. Add the mashed bananas and self-raising flour. Stir gently until well mixed.
4. Add the peanuts and mix well.
5. Grease two loaf pans and divide the mixture between them.
6. Bake in an oven until golden brown.

Breadfruit

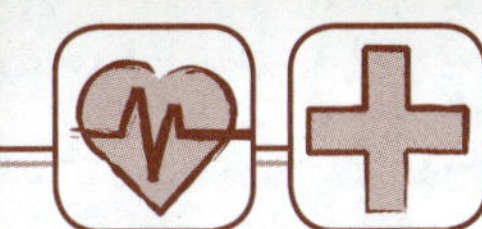

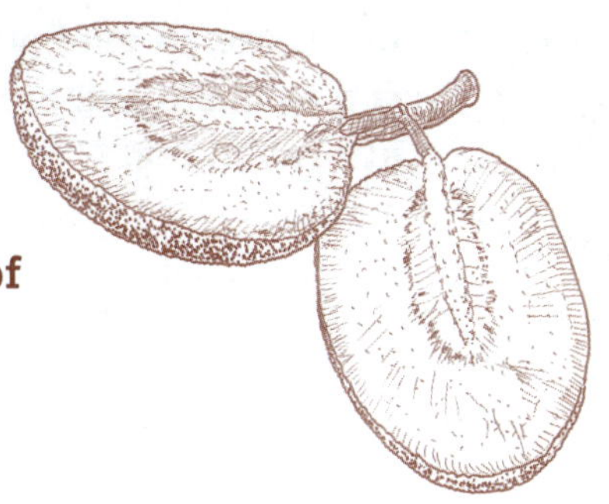

The fruit of the breadfruit is an energy food and also contains some Vitamin B1 and Vitamin C. The food value of the flesh is similar to that of sweet potato, but the seeds contain more protein and are similar to the food value of nuts.

Some varieties of breadfruit have very few seeds. The flesh of the fruit is roasted or boiled before it is eaten. Other varieties of breadfruit are full of seeds and have very little flesh. The seeds are roasted or boiled before they are eaten.

Breadfruit chips

INGREDIENTS

1 firm breadfruit

oil for frying

salt to taste

PROCEDURE

1. Peel the breadfruit and cut it into quarters.
2. Take out the middle core.
3. Slice the quarters into very thin slices.
4. Heat the oil in a frying pan and fry the slices quickly until crisp.
5. Drain the chips and sprinkle with salt to taste.

Breadfruit fritters

INGREDIENTS

1 firm breadfruit

2 cups of plain flour

salt to taste

crushed ginger

crushed garlic

1 teaspoon of curry powder (or 1 chicken cube)

1 cup of water

oil for frying

PROCEDURE

1. Peel the breadfruit and cut it in half. Take out the core.
2. Slice the halves into thin slices that are slightly thicker than chips.
3. Mix the flour, salt, ginger and garlic in a dish. Add the curry powder or chicken cube and mix well.
4. Add just enough water to make a batter that will coat the slices of breadfruit.
5. Dip slices of breadfruit into this batter, a few pieces at a time, and fry until golden brown.
6. Drain on paper towels. Serve hot.

Cakes

Cakes are an energy food. They are easy and fun to make and are great for morning and afternoon tea.

Plain cake

INGREDIENTS

$\frac{3}{4}$ cup of sugar

2 eggs

$\frac{1}{4}$ cup of butter

1 teaspoon of vanilla

$1\frac{1}{2}$ cups of self-raising flour

$\frac{1}{2}$ cup of milk

PROCEDURE

1. Cream the sugar and eggs until smooth.
2. Melt the butter.
3. Add the melted butter and vanilla to the sugar and eggs.
4. Sift the flour and add it to the mixture. Add the milk and mix well.
5. Grease a cake tin and pour the mixture into the tin.
6. Bake until golden brown.

Banana cake

INGREDIENTS

1 cup of butter or margarine

1 egg

3 tablespoons of coconut milk

1 cup of sugar

1½ cups of self-raising flour

2 mashed bananas

PROCEDURE

1. Cream the butter and sugar until very smooth.
2. Beat the egg and fold it into the butter and sugar mixture.
3. Add half of the self-raising flour and fold it into the mixture.
4. Add the milk, the mashed bananas and the rest of the flour. Mix gently until combined.
5. Pour the mixture into a greased 20 cm (8 inch) cake tin. Bake in a moderate oven for 30 minutes or until golden brown.

Coconut cream cake

INGREDIENTS

2 cups of self-raising flour

1 small coconut

½ cup of oil

1 teaspoon of vanilla

½ teaspoon of salt

1 cup of sugar

2 eggs

PROCEDURE

1. Sift the flour and salt. Put aside.
2. Grate the coconut. Squeeze the coconut milk into a cup and add water to make a full cup.
3. Mix the sugar, oil, eggs, vanilla and coconut milk together. Beat well.
4. Add the flour and gently mix until smooth.
5. Pour the mixture into a greased pan and bake for about 25–30 minutes.

Cassava
(tapioca)

Cassava (tapioca) is a small shrub. It is common in many areas because it gets little pest or disease damage. The tubers contain starch and therefore they are an energy food. The leaves are high in Vitamin A content and relatively high in protein as well.

Note: The raw tubers and leaves contain small amounts of poisonous chemicals. Tubers must be soaked in water for a long time before cooking to remove these poisonous substances.

Cassava wrapped in banana leaves

INGREDIENTS

4 medium-sized pieces of cassava

3 aibika leaves

salt to taste

banana leaves for wrapping

3 ripe bananas

½ tin of fish or ½ fresh fish

1 mature coconut

PROCEDURE

1. Clear and prepare a mumu pit. Arrange a layer of stones on the bottom of the pit. Make a small fire on top of these stones. Wait for the fire to burn itself out and the stones to become very hot. This will take about an hour. Meanwhile, soak the cassava in water.
2. Peel and wash the cassava. Grate it into a dish and pour off any liquid.
3. Slice the ripe bananas.
4. Wash the aibika leaves and cut them up finely.
5. Mix the cassava, bananas, aibika and fish together with a fork. Sprinkle on some salt.
6. Scrape the coconut and squeeze out the coconut cream.

Cassava wrapped in banana leaves (continued)

7 Mix the coconut cream into the cassava mixture.
8 Prepare the banana leaf wraps by cutting off the hard stem and holding the leaf over the hot stones until the leaf becomes soft. Remove the leaf from the stones.
9 Place a handful of the cassava mixture onto a square of banana leaf and wrap into a flat parcel. Tie the parcel. Repeat until all the mixture has been used.
10 Place the cassava wraps on the stones and cover them with more hot stones, making sure that each parcel has hot stones surrounding it.
11 Cover the pit with banana leaves to prevent the steam from escaping and cook the wraps for 60–90 minutes.
12 Remove the leaf wrappings before serving.

Note: *This dish can be eaten hot or cold.*

Cassava chips

INGREDIENTS

2 cassava

oil for frying

salt to taste

PROCEDURE

1 Soak the cassava in water.
2 Peel the cassava and boil until it is almost cooked but still firm. Leave to cool.
3 Thinly slice the cassava.
4 Heat the oil and fry the cassava slices until crisp.
5 Drain on paper towels and sprinkle with salt.

Note: *Leftover cassava is excellent for making chips.*
Serve as a snack or a light lunch.

Chicken

Poultry, especially chicken, is a very good source of protein. Chickens are now being kept in most villages for food and eggs. It is important that people care for chickens properly. Chickens that only rely on the food they find around the village are very thin and are a bit tougher to eat. They also often get diseases and normally lay fewer eggs.

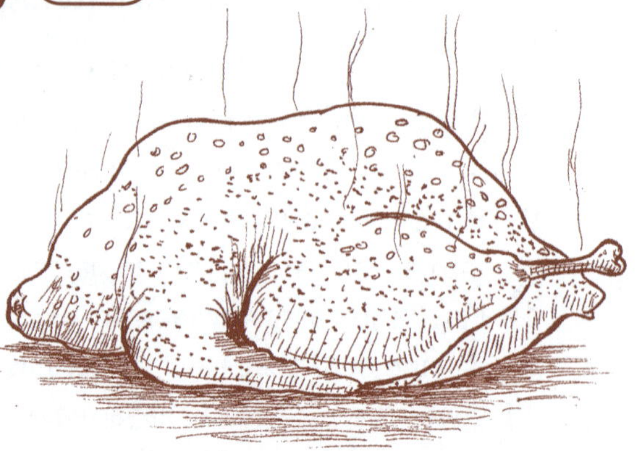

Chicken fingers

INGREDIENTS

1 cup of plain flour

1 chicken cube

¼ cup of milk or cold water

oil for frying

1 teaspoon of baking powder

salt to taste

2 chicken breasts

PROCEDURE

1. Put the flour, baking powder, crushed chicken cube and salt in a dish and mix well.
2. Add water or milk and stir to form a smooth paste.
3. Cut the chicken breasts into fingers.
4. Heat the oil in a frying pan. Dip the pieces of chicken in the batter and fry over a medium heat until golden brown.

Note: *If you want a spicy batter, add crushed garlic, ginger and chilli or any other herbs to the flour.*
This recipe is nice with fried taro, tapioca or yams.

Chicken pieces

INGREDIENTS

1 piece of ginger
3 large carrots
1 cup of plain flour
salt to taste
2 tablespoons of oil
1 extra tablespoon of plain flour
3 medium-sized capsicums
4–5 spring onions
1 chicken cube
chicken pieces
2 cups of warm water

PROCEDURE

1. Clean and crush the ginger.
2. Wash and dice the capsicums and carrots.
3. Wash and chop the spring onions.
4. Put 1 cup of the flour in a dish with the crushed chicken cube and salt. Mix well.
5. Coat the chicken pieces in the flour mixture.
6. Heat the oil in a frying pan and fry the chicken pieces until golden brown. When cooked, remove the chicken pieces from the pan.
7. Drain the excess oil from the frying pan. Add the crushed ginger and fry until golden brown.
8. Add the capsicums, carrots and chicken. Cook for a few minutes.
9. Stir in the spring onions and salt to taste. Add 2 cups of warm water.
10. Mix 1 tablespoon of flour in a little bit of cold water and add to the chicken mixture. Stir well.
11. Cook over a low heat until the carrots and capsicums are just done. Don't overcook.

Note: *Serve this dish with rice, sweet potato, banana or tapioca.*

Chicken with vegetables and noodles

INGREDIENTS

2 chicken breasts

2 tablespoons of oil

2 cups of finely chopped cabbage

1 packet of dried noodles

2 dessertspoons of plain flour

1 piece of ginger

2 sliced carrots

3 chopped shallots

1 cup of water

PROCEDURE

1. Cut the chicken breasts into thin slices.
2. Clean and crush the ginger.
3. Heat the oil in a saucepan. Add the ginger and fry until golden brown.
4. Add the chicken and cook for about 3–4 minutes. Stir every now and then.
5. Add the sliced carrots and stir for a minute. Add the cabbage, shallots and noodles. Stir well.
6. Add the flavouring from the noodle packet.
7. Mix 2 dessertspoons of flour in a cup of water and pour it over the vegetables and chicken. Stir well.
8. Cook until the vegetables are tender and the noodles are cooked.

Note: *This mixture can be eaten alone or with rice or any boiled root crop. Very tasty!*

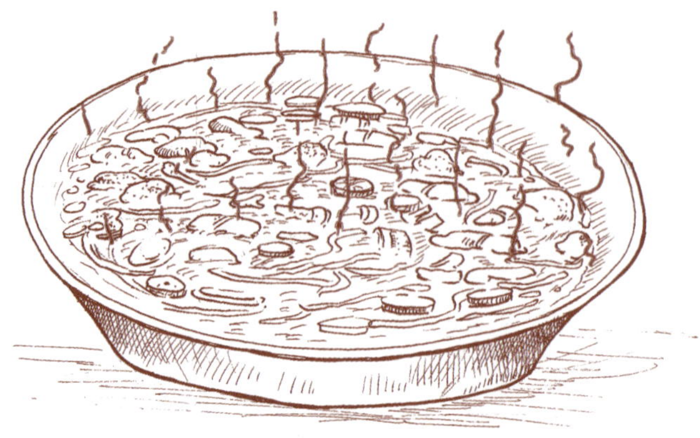

Coconut

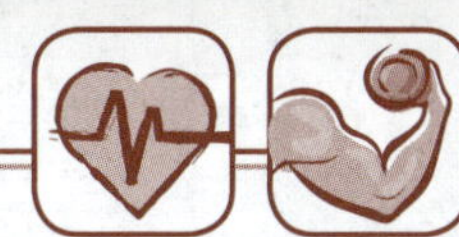

The flesh of ripe coconuts is mainly used to give flavour to other foods, but it is also a good food itself. It is an energy food because of the fat it contains. It also has a small amount of protein.

The water from young green coconuts, called *kulau*, provides a good clean source of liquid for drinking and cooking. It is also a good source of Vitamin B.

Green coconuts can be picked from the tree after careful climbing. Mature coconuts will fall to the ground when they are ripe.

Meal in a coconut shell

INGREDIENTS

4 sweet potatoes

1 tomato

¼ small pineapple

½ cup of coconut milk

2 spring onions

½ cup of any edible green leaves

1 coconut

PROCEDURE

1. Peel and wash the sweet potatoes. Cut into small pieces.
2. Wash and chop the spring onions, tomato and green leaves. Chop the pineapple.
3. Line the inside of half of a coconut shell with some of the green leaves.
4. Place all the vegetables inside the shell.
5. Pour the coconut milk over the vegetables.
6. Cover with more green leaves. Put the other half of the coconut shell on top and tie tightly in place.
7. Boil the shell in a pan of water for about 45 minutes.
8. Open the shell and serve hot.

Eggplant

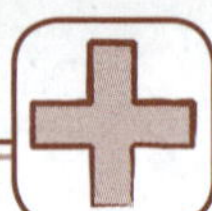

Eggplant is a tropical plant with spreading branches bearing egg-shaped fruit that is white or dark purple in colour and is eaten as a vegetable. Eggplant is rich in vitamins and minerals. There are a number of varieties of eggplant in Papua New Guinea.

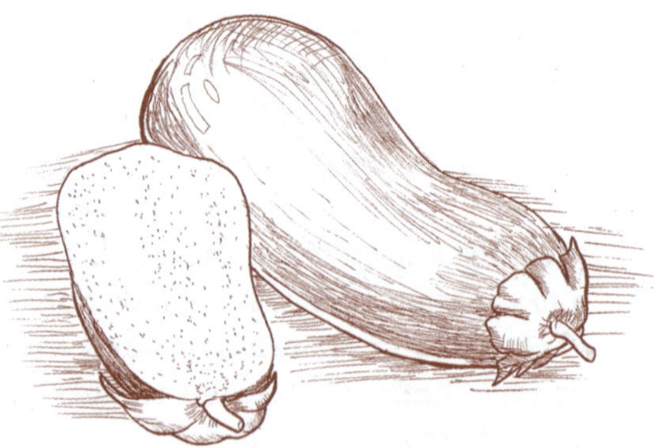

Eggplant and green peppers

INGREDIENTS

4–5 medium-sized eggplants

3 medium-sized green capsicums

oil for frying

1 teaspoon of turmeric

1 teaspoon of garam masala

5 medium-sized tomatoes

1 large onion

1 piece of crushed ginger

salt to taste

PROCEDURE

1. Wash the eggplants, tomatoes and green peppers.
2. Cut the eggplants into 5 cm (2 inch) pieces in water.
3. Cut the tomatoes into quarters. Slice the green capsicums.
4. Finely slice the onion.
5. Heat the oil and fry the onions and ginger until tender.
6. Add the eggplant, turmeric and salt and fry for 5–10 minutes.
7. Add the tomatoes and green peppers. Stir well, cover and cook until the eggplants are tender.
8. Sprinkle the garam masala over the mixture and cook over a low heat for another 2–3 minutes.

Fried eggplant

INGREDIENTS

3 large eggplants

2 teaspoons of turmeric

salt to taste

oil for frying

PROCEDURE

1 Wash the eggplants and cut them into thick round slices.
2 Marinate the eggplant slices in a mixture of turmeric and salt and leave for an hour.
3 Press the eggplant slices between your hands to remove excess moisture.
4 Heat the oil in a frying pan and fry the eggplant slices on both sides.

Eggplant and potatoes

INGREDIENTS

1 medium-sized onion or several spring onions

6 medium-sized potatoes

¼ cup of oil

1 teaspoon of turmeric

salt to taste

2 medium-sized tomatoes

4 medium-sized eggplants

1 small piece of ginger

1 teaspoon of garam masala

1 teaspoon of chilli powder

PROCEDURE

1 Slice the onion or spring onions.
2 Slice the tomatoes, potatoes and eggplants.
3 Heat the oil in a deep frying pan. Fry the onion and ginger for a few minutes.
4 Add the turmeric, garam masala, salt and chilli powder. Cook for a few minutes, stirring well.
5 Add the tomatoes and fry for a few minutes until the tomato juice has almost dried up.
6 Add the potatoes and eggplant to this mixture. Mix well.
7 Cook the curry on a medium heat until the vegetables are tender.

Fish

Fish is high in protein and is a body-building food.

Fresh fish must be cleaned and cooked. Tinned fish can be used instead of fresh fish in areas such as the Highlands where people cannot catch fish. Dried fish is also useful as it can be stored for many months.

Spicy coconut fish

INGREDIENTS

½ kg (1 lb) of fish

3 onions

1 green capsicum

3 tablespoons of oil

2 cups of thick coconut milk

salt to taste

juice of 1 lemon

PROCEDURE

1. Clean the fish and cut it into slices.
2. Chop the onions and green capsicum.
3. Fry the fish in some of the oil, then remove from the pan.
4. Fry the chopped onion and green pepper until the onions are soft.
5. Add the fish, coconut milk and salt.
6. Cover and cook on a low heat until the fish is cooked.
7. Add the lemon juice before serving.

Fried floured fish

INGREDIENTS

½ kg (1 lb) of fish

salt to taste

¼ teaspoon of chilli powder (optional)

oil for frying

1 lemon

4–5 crushed garlic cloves

1 cup of plain flour

PROCEDURE

1. Clean and slice the fish.
2. Put the fish in a dish and coat the fish with lemon juice, salt, garlic and chilli powder (if using). Let it stand for half an hour.

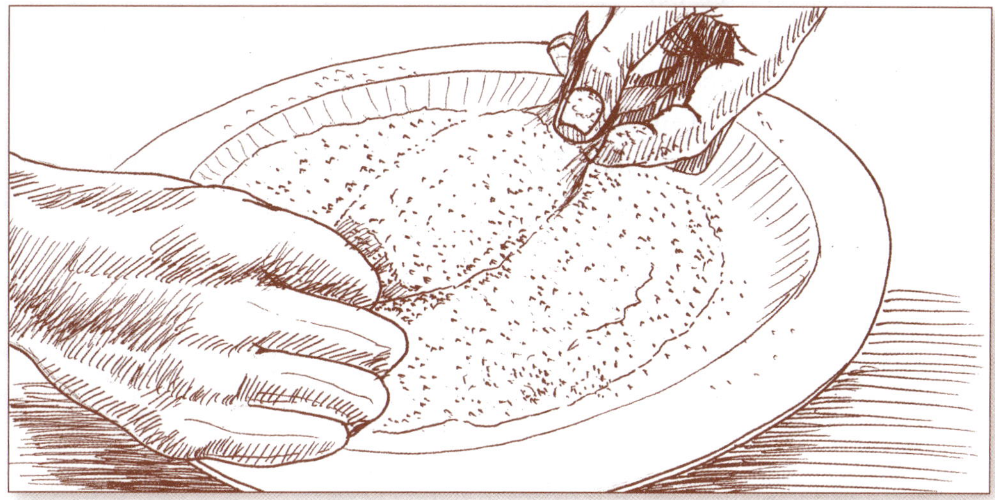

3. Put the flour in a dish and coat each piece of fish in the flour.
4. Heat the oil in a frying pan. Fry the fish over gentle heat until it is golden brown in colour.

Note: *Serve this fish with vegetables such as sweet potato, taro, yams or bananas.*

Fried fish in coconut cream

INGREDIENTS

½ kg (1 lb) of fish

salt to taste

¼ teaspoon of chilli powder (optional)

oil for frying

2 tomatoes

2 cups of thick coconut cream

juice of 1 lemon

4–5 crushed garlic cloves

1 cup of plain flour

1 onion

1 piece of ginger

PROCEDURE

1. Clean and slice the fish.
2. Put the fish in a dish and coat with the lemon juice, salt, garlic and chilli powder (if using). Let it stand for half an hour.
3. Put the flour in a dish and coat each piece of fish in the flour.
4. Heat the oil in a frying pan. Fry the fish pieces over a gentle heat until the fish is golden brown in colour.
5. Chop the onion and tomatoes and crush the ginger.
6. Put the fried fish into a saucepan and add the coconut cream, onion, tomatoes and ginger.
7. Cook until the coconut cream is absorbed into the fish.

 **Note:** *This is a delicious recipe!*

Fish curry

INGREDIENTS

salt to taste

½ teaspoon of turmeric

1 kg (2 lbs) of fish fillets

1 lemon

2 chopped onions

2 teaspoons of grated ginger

6–7 crushed garlic cloves

several chopped chillies (optional)

¼ cup of oil for frying

PROCEDURE

1. Mix together the salt and turmeric and rub into the fish.
2. Squeeze the lemon over the fish and allow to marinate for at least 2 hours.
3. Mash together the onions, ginger, garlic and chopped chillies (if using). Heat the oil in a saucepan and fry the onion mixture.
4. Add the fish, cover with water and cook over a low heat until the fish is tender.

Uncooked tinned fish

INGREDIENTS

1 large tin of Besta
(with or without tomatoes)

1 onion

2 medium-sized tomatoes

1 large carrot

2 cups of sliced round cabbage

salt to taste

PROCEDURE

1. Open the tin, put the fish in a dish and scrape out the soft black skin, taking out the soft bones. Break the fish into pieces.
2. Slice the onion, chop the tomatoes and grate the carrot. Gently mix these vegetables with the fish.
3. Add the cabbage and sprinkle with salt. Mix well.

Note: *Spring onion can be used instead of round onion. Add a dessertspoon of lemon juice if desired. Eat this dish with sweet potato, bananas or sago.*

Tinned fish for sandwiches

INGREDIENTS

1 large carrot
2–3 shallots
1 large tin of Besta
1 teaspoon of curry powder (optional)
2 cups of grated or finely chopped cabbage
1 cucumber
salt to taste

PROCEDURE

1 Wash and grate the carrot and cabbage.
2 Finely chop the shallots. Peel and thinly slice the cucumber.
3 Open the tin of fish and scrape out the bones and black skin on top. Put the fish into a saucepan and break it into pieces.
4 Add the cabbage and curry powder (if using). Stir well, then cover the pan and cook for 5 minutes.
5 Add the carrot, shallots and salt and mix well.
6 To serve, spread the mixture on bread and place the cucumber slices on top.

Note: *This mixture can also be eaten with sweet potato or bananas.*

Tinned fish with round cabbage

INGREDIENTS

1 small round cabbage
several garlic cloves
3 tablespoons of oil
1 large tin of Besta
(with tomatoes or with oil)
1 small onion
1 piece of ginger
2 tablespoons of curry powder (optional)
salt to taste

PROCEDURE

1 Finely chop the cabbage.
2 Slice the onion and crush the garlic and ginger.
3 Heat the oil in a frying pan. Add the garlic and ginger and fry for a few minutes until golden brown.
4 Add the cabbage and curry powder (if using). Stir well, then cover the pan and cook for 5 minutes.
5 Open the tin of fish, take out the soft bones and scrape the black skin off the fish.

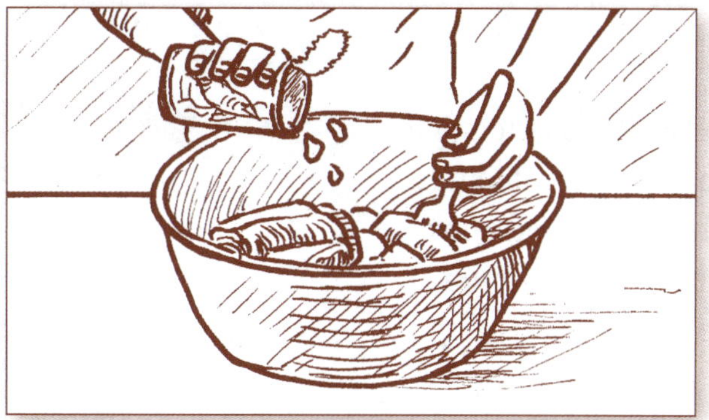

6 Break the fish into pieces and add to the cabbage mixture. Add salt to taste.
7 Cook for a further 5 minutes.

Note: *Serve with rice, sweet potato or bananas.*

Tinned fish with tomatoes

INGREDIENTS

1 large tin of Besta with oil

3 large tomatoes

3 shallots

1 piece of ginger

4–5 cloves of garlic

3 tablespoons of oil

salt to taste

PROCEDURE

1. Open the tin of fish and remove the bones and black skin.
2. Chop the tomatoes and shallots.
3. Crush the ginger and garlic and fry in the oil for a few minutes.
4. Add the tomatoes, shallots and salt and cook for 3–4 minutes.
5. Add the tinned fish and cook for a further 5 minutes on a medium heat.

Note: *This recipe is delicious. It can be used as a sandwich filling and eaten with Indian bread.*

Fish balls

INGREDIENTS

1 small tin of Besta or tuna

1 cup of mashed potato

1 chopped onion

½ cup of flour

salt to taste

oil for frying

PROCEDURE

1. Open the tin of fish and scrape out the bones and the black skin.
2. Mix all ingredients together.
3. Roll into balls and dust with flour.
4. Heat the oil in a frying pan and fry the balls until golden brown.

Note: *These balls are very tasty!*

Peanuts

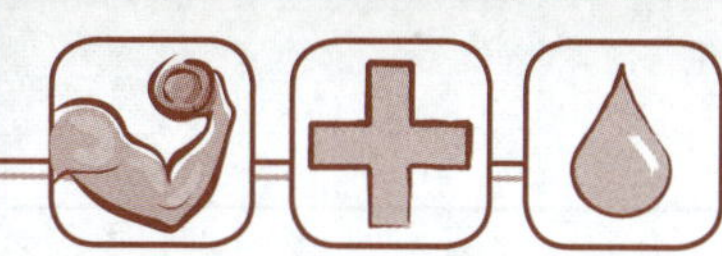

The peanut's main food value is protein. Peanuts contain a lot of fat and therefore you only need to eat a small amount to get a large amount of energy. Peanuts are also rich in Vitamins B and E.

Peanuts are easy to cook. They can be added to mixed vegetables, stews and meat. They can also be roasted on a sheet of iron over a fire in their shells and fried in oil.

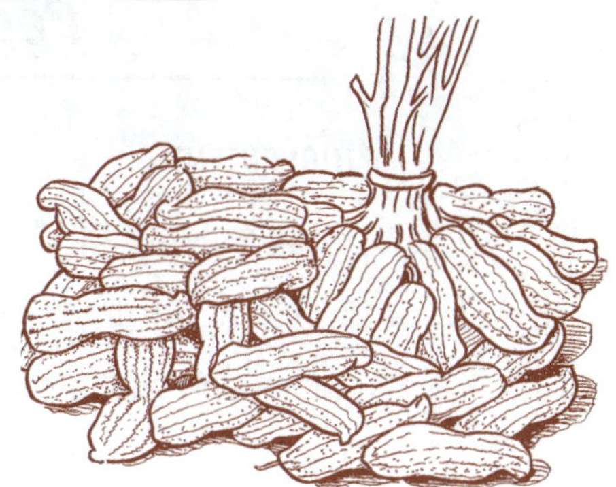

Peanuts and rice

INGREDIENTS

3 cups of rice	¼ cup of margarine or oil
1 sliced spring onion	1 sliced onion
1 cup of diced carrots	1 cup of green peas
¾ cup of fried peanuts	salt to taste

PROCEDURE

1. Soak the rice in water for 15 minutes, then drain.
2. Heat the margarine or oil. Add the rice and fry on a medium heat for a few minutes.
3. Add the vegetables and peanuts and mix well.
4. Add 6 cups of water and bring to the boil. Turn down the heat and cook until the rice is soft.

Note: *To avoid overcooking the vegetables, you can add them once the rice is half cooked.*

Peanuts and oxen palm

INGREDIENTS

2 tablespoons of oil

1 cup of cut green beans

2 chopped shallots

1 packet of dried noodles

1 tin of oxen palm

1 piece of crushed ginger

1 cup of diced carrots

1 cup of shelled, fried peanuts

2 cups of finely chopped cabbage

PROCEDURE

1 Heat the oil in a frying pan and fry the ginger for a few minutes.
2 Add the beans, carrots and shallots and stir for a few minutes.
3 Add the peanuts and stir again.
4 Break the noodles and add them to the fried vegetables. Stir over a low heat for a few minutes.

5 Add the cabbage and oxen palm and cook for another 3–4 minutes.

Note: *This is a delicious dish that can be eaten with anything. If using raw peanuts, fry them before using in this recipe.*

Peanuts and stir-fried vegetables

INGREDIENTS

3 tablespoons of oil

crushed ginger and garlic

2 cups of sliced carrots

1 cup of green peas

1 cup of fried peanuts

3 sliced capsicums

3 chopped shallots

2 cups of finely chopped cabbage

PROCEDURE

1. Heat the oil in a frying pan to a medium heat.
2. Add the crushed ginger and garlic and fry until it turns a light colour.
3. Add the carrots and green peas and stir well, then add the peanuts.
4. Add the rest of the vegetables and fry until the vegetables are cooked.

Note: *This dish should be served hot. Any vegetables can be used in this recipe.*

Peanut butter

INGREDIENTS

1 cup of peanuts

2–3 tablespoons of oil

1 small spoonful of salt

PROCEDURE

1. Crush the peanuts with a stone on a chopping board.

2. Add oil gradually while crushing the peanuts, then add salt.

Note: *If using raw peanuts, fry them and remove the skins before crushing. To eat, spread this mixture on any type of bread.*

Potato (European)

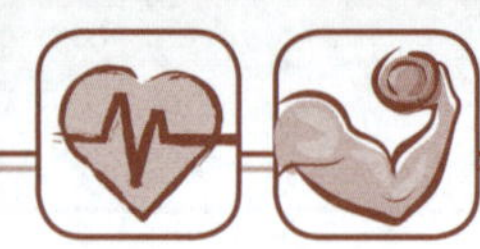

European potato contains much more protein than sweet potato and can be promoted as a useful addition to the diet. The European potato was introduced to Papua New Guinea and grows very well in the Highlands. It grows faster than sweet potato and can give good yields if healthy planting stock is used.

If stored correctly, European potatoes can be kept much longer than sweet potatoes.

Potato curry with tomatoes (spicy)

INGREDIENTS

½ kg (1 lb) of potatoes
½ cup of oil
1 teaspoon of turmeric
salt to taste
2 large tomatoes
1 teaspoon of cumin seeds
1 teaspoon of chilli

PROCEDURE

1 Peel and dice the potatoes.
2 Chop the tomatoes.
3 Heat the oil and add the potatoes, cumin seeds, turmeric, chilli and salt. Fry for about 2–3 minutes.
4 Stir the mixture, then add chopped tomatoes and cook on a medium heat.
5 When the potatoes start to stick to the frying pan, add just enough hot water to cover the potatoes.
6 Cook until the potatoes are well done.

Note: *This recipe is like potatoes with thick gravy.*

Potato curry (dry)

INGREDIENTS

½ kg (1 lb) of small potatoes

1 onion

¼ cup of oil

1 teaspoon of curry powder

chilli (optional)

salt to taste

PROCEDURE

1 Peel the potatoes. If they are large, cut them into halves and quarters.

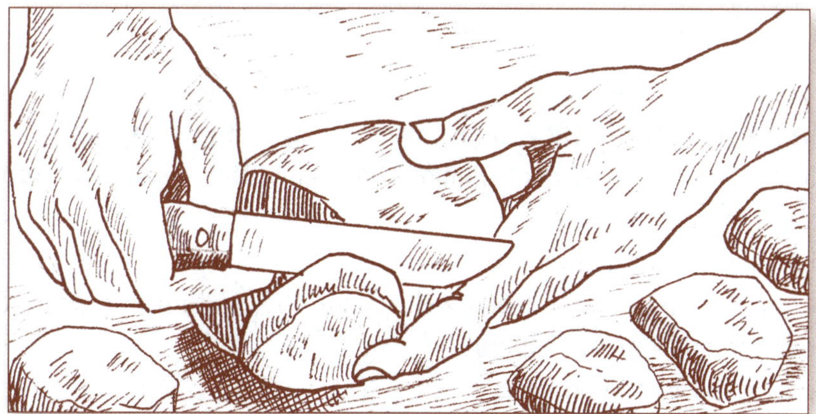

2 Chop the onion.

3 Heat the oil in a saucepan and gently fry the onion.

4 Add the curry powder, chilli (if using) and salt. Mix well.

5 Add the potatoes. Stir for a few minutes and then turn the heat down to low.

6 Cook with the lid on for 30 minutes or until the potato is tender.

Note: *If the potatoes begin to stick to the pan, add a little water and stir. Serve with roti or puri.*

Potato balls

INGREDIENTS

4–5 medium-sized potatoes

salt to taste

2 teaspoons of crushed garlic

½ cup of plain flour

1 piece of ginger

2 tablespoons of finely chopped coriander or other herbs

¼ teaspoon of chilli powder (optional)

1 beaten egg

oil for frying

PROCEDURE

1. Boil the potatoes in their skins until the skins start to split.
2. Allow the potatoes to cool. Remove the skins, then mash the potatoes to make a smooth mixture.
3. Add the salt, garlic, flour, ginger, herbs and chilli powder (if using) to the potato mixture and knead well. Shape the mixture into small balls.
4. Break the egg into a dish and beat well.
5. Heat the oil in a deep pan.
6. Coat the potato balls in the beaten egg and drop into the hot oil. You can drop 3–4 balls in at the same time. Fry until golden brown.
7. Drain the balls and serve either hot or cold.

Note: *You can use finely chopped fresh young curry leaves instead of coriander.*

Sago

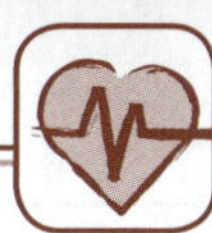

Sago is an energy food. It has no other food value. Sago starch is a very bulky food because it contains a lot of water. It is important to supplement the sago with other foods such as fish or green leaves, which contain protein and vitamins. If sago is the main food eaten, it is difficult for people, especially children, to obtain enough energy to meet their daily requirements.

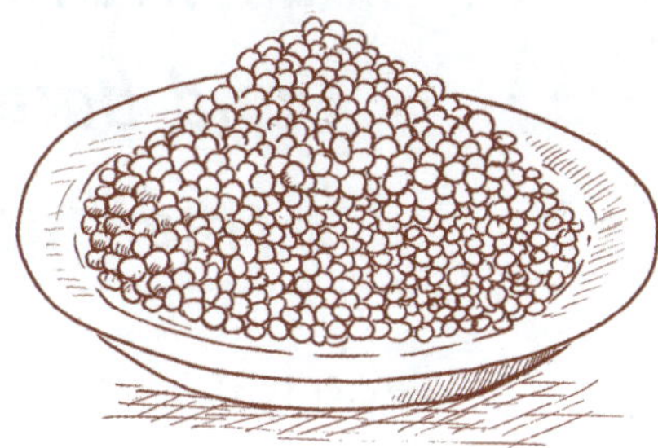

The sago palm grows wild in the swampy lowland areas of Papua New Guinea. The sago starch that is used as food comes from the inside of the trunks of the palms.

Sago with coconut and bananas (method 1)

INGREDIENTS

2 cups of sago	3/4 cup of mashed ripe banana
2 coconuts	1 cup of warm water

PROCEDURE

1. Put the sago in a dish and break up any lumps. Add the banana and mix well.
2. Scrape the coconuts. Add 1 cup of warm water and squeeze out the coconut milk by pouring through a strainer.
3. Pour 3 cups of water into a large saucepan and bring to the boil.
4. Drop spoonfuls of the sago mixture into the boiling water. Cover the saucepan with the lid and boil the sago for about 10 minutes or until it is cooked. Stir occasionally so that the sago doesn't stick to the bottom of the saucepan.
5. Pour the coconut milk into the sago mixture and stir gently until the coconut milk is heated through.

Note: *The sago will turn a brownish colour when cooked. This dish should be served cold.*

Sago with coconut and bananas (method 2)

INGREDIENTS

2 cups of sago

1 cup of scraped coconut

½ cup of mashed ripe banana

oil for frying

PROCEDURE

1. Put the sago in a dish and break up any lumps.
2. Add the coconut and banana. Mix well.
3. Heat the oil in a frying pan.
4. Form the sago mixture into balls and drop them into the hot oil.
5. Fry until golden brown.
6. Drain well before serving.

Note: *This dish can be eaten hot or cold.*

Sago and sweet potato

INGREDIENTS

2 cups of sago

½ cup of scraped coconut

1 cup of mashed sweet potato

oil for frying

PROCEDURE

1. Put the sago in a dish and break up any lumps.
2. Add the coconut and sweet potato. Mix well.
3. Heat the oil in a frying pan.
4. Form the sago mixture into little balls and fry until brown.

Note: *This dish should be served warm.*

Sago pancakes

INGREDIENTS

2 cups of sago

3 teaspoons of sugar

1 cup of ripe mashed banana

oil for frying

PROCEDURE

1 Put the sago into a dish and rub it between your fingers to smooth out all lumps.

2 Add the banana and sugar and mix well.

3 Heat the oil in a flat frying pan on a medium heat.

4 Drop spoonfuls of the mixture into the oil a few at a time. Flatten the drops a little bit as you place them in the frying pan.

5 Cook for a few minutes, then turn over and cook the other side.

6 Drain well and serve.

 **Note:** *These pancakes can be eaten hot or cold.*

Scones

Scones are an energy food. Many different vegetables can be used to make different types of scones. Scones can be served for morning or afternoon tea or eaten with an evening dish instead of bread.

Frying pan scones

INGREDIENTS

2 cups of plain flour

2 teaspoons of baking powder

½ teaspoon of salt

2 tablespoons of butter

coconut milk to mix

oil for frying

PROCEDURE

1. Sift the flour, baking powder and salt.
2. Using your fingers, gently rub the butter into the flour mixture.
3. Add enough coconut milk to make a soft dough (don't knead too much).
4. Grease a round flat frying pan. Roll the scone mixture into the size and shape of the frying pan.
5. Cook the scone on a gentle heat for roughly 5 minutes on each side.
6. Cut the scone into squares and serve hot with butter and jam.

Plain scones

INGREDIENTS

3 cups of plain flour

3 teaspoons of baking powder

¼ cup of butter

½ teaspoon of salt

1 cup of milk

PROCEDURE

1. Sift the flour and baking powder into a bowl.
2. Using your fingers, gently rub the butter into the flour.
3. Dissolve the salt in the milk and add to the flour.
4. Mix to a soft dough and knead lightly on a floured board.
5. Roll out the dough, cut into small rounds and place on a greased floured tray.
6. Bake for around 10–15 minutes or until golden brown.

Pumpkin scones

INGREDIENTS

1 tablespoon of melted butter

½ cup of sugar

½ cup of cold water

1 egg

1 cup of cold mashed pumpkin

2 cups of self-raising flour

½ teaspoon of salt

PROCEDURE

1. Blend the butter and sugar with the water.
2. Beat the egg and pumpkin together.
3. Sift the flour and salt.
4. Combine all the ingredients and mix gently until well blended.
5. Form pieces of the dough into scones and place on a greased floured tray. Bake for 10–15 minutes.

Note: *Any cold vegetable, such as banana, eggplant or sweet potato, can be used to make savoury scones.*

Sweet potato

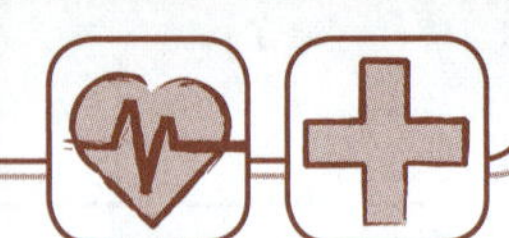

The sweet potato is a trailing vine that grows tubers under the ground. Both the tubers and the young leaves can be eaten. The tubers are starchy and are an energy food. The young leaves contain vitamins and can be eaten as a protective food.

Sweet potato can be grown almost everywhere in Papua New Guinea, even in very high altitude areas. Each part of Papua New Guinea has its own favourite kind of sweet potato. It is estimated that there are over 500 different varieties of sweet potato in Papua New Guinea.

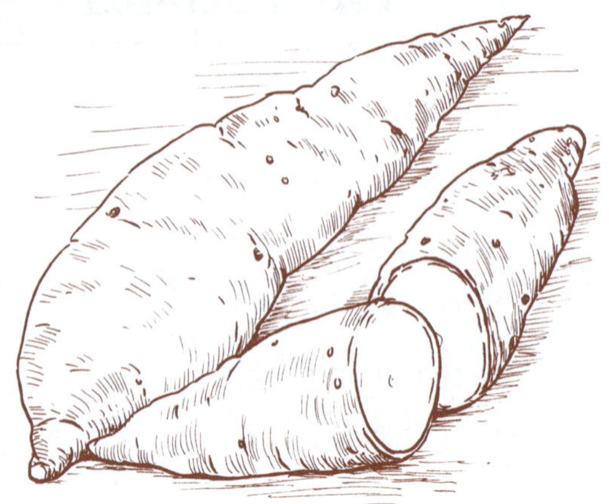

Sweet potato biscuits

INGREDIENTS

- 1 cup of plain flour
- pinch of salt
- ½ cup of mashed cooked sweet potato
- 1 teaspoon of baking powder
- ¼ cup of sugar
- 2 tablespoons of margarine
- 1 tablespoon of milk

PROCEDURE

1. Sift the flour, baking powder and salt into a bowl. Add the sugar.
2. Mix the sweet potato with the margarine and milk.
3. Add the flour mixture to the sweet potato mixture and mix into a soft dough.
4. Take small spoonfuls of the dough and roll into balls. Place close together on a greased tray. Press the balls down lightly with a fork.
5. Bake in a moderate oven for around 15 minutes.

Note: *Store biscuits in an airtight container.*

Sweet potato and pineapple casserole

INGREDIENTS

4 medium-sized sweet potatoes

1 grated coconut

4 tablespoons of butter

1 sliced pineapple

PROCEDURE

1 Boil the unpeeled sweet potatoes until tender.
2 Drain the sweet potatoes, peel them and slice into pieces about 1 cm (½ inch) thick.
3 Grease a baking dish and sprinkle with grated coconut.
4 Dot with small pieces of butter.
5 Arrange a layer of pineapple in the baking dish.
6 Top with a layer of sweet potato.
7 Repeat these layers until all the sweet potato and pineapple has been used.
8 Bake in a hot oven for about 30 minutes.

Sweet potato with peanuts

INGREDIENTS

3 medium-sized sweet potatoes

1 tablespoon of brown sugar

1 tablespoon of butter or margarine

¼ cup of peanuts

PROCEDURE

1 Bake the sweet potatoes in the ashes of a fire or in an oven.
2 Cut each sweet potato in half.
3 Mix the sugar, butter and peanuts in a pan and cook for 10 minutes.
4 Place 2 teaspoons of this mixture on top of each sweet potato half and serve immediately.

Note: *Serve this dish with green leaves and other cooked vegetables.*

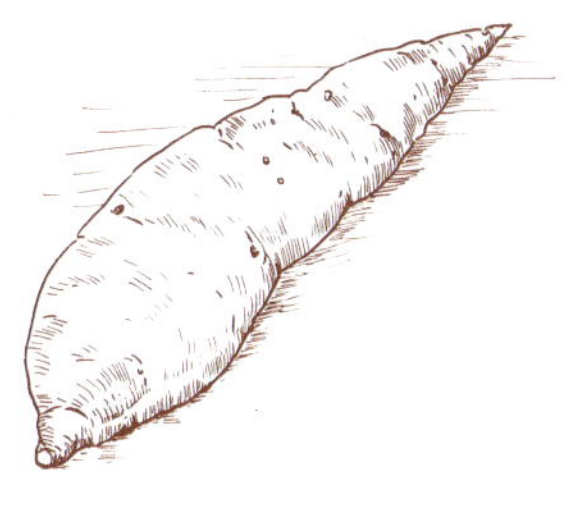

Taro

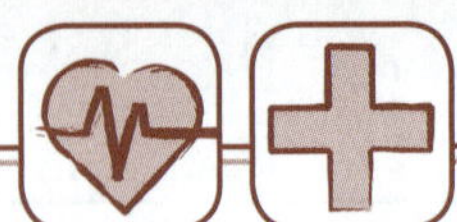

There are four different types of taro commonly eaten in Papua New Guinea, but the most popular is common taro. The underground tuber of the plant is eaten as well as the young leaves and stems of the leaves. The tuber is starchy and is an energy food. The young leaves and stems are full of vitamins and minerals.

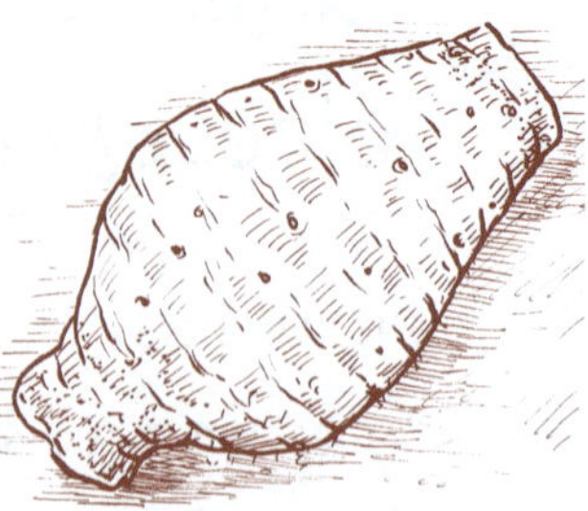

Taro and meat curry

INGREDIENTS

2 small taros
1 tomato
2 teaspoons of margarine
salt to taste
1 onion
2 tins of sliced meat
1 teaspoon curry powder
2 ripe bananas

PROCEDURE

1. Wash and peel the taros and cut into pieces.
2. Put the taro pieces in a saucepan of water and boil until soft.
3. Wash the onion and tomato and cut into small pieces.
4. Chop the meat into pieces.
5. Heat the margarine in a saucepan and fry the onion, tomato and meat.
6. Stir in the curry powder and salt. Add a little water to prevent the mixture from burning.
7. Cut the bananas into slices.
8. To serve, put the taro on a plate and pour the meat sauce over the taro. Arrange the slices of banana on top.

Taro chips

INGREDIENTS

several taros
oil for frying
salt to taste

PROCEDURE

1 Boil the taros until almost cooked but not too soft. Leave to cool.
2 Slice the taros into thin slices and fry in hot oil until crisp.
3 Sprinkle with salt and eat immediately.

Note: *Another way of making these chips is to make a batter with just enough flour with salt to cover the amount of sliced taro.*

1 Boil the taros until almost cooked but not too soft. Leave to cool, then slice thinly.
2 Add crushed garlic and ginger to flour, then mix with water to make a thick batter.
3 Dip the taro slices into this batter and fry until golden brown.
4 Drain well and serve hot.

Note: *Remember to add ½ teaspoon of baking powder to each cup of flour.*

Tea time varieties

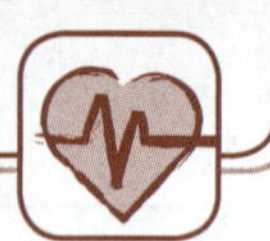

These sweet and savoury bites are great for afternoon tea. They are easy to make and can be eaten hot or cold.

Coconut puffs (sweet)

INGREDIENTS

3 cups of plain flour

1 teaspoon of baking powder

½ cup of sugar

1 cup of coconut cream

2 tablespoons of oil

PROCEDURE

1 Mix the flour, baking powder, sugar and coconut cream together and knead into a dough.

2 Let the dough rest for 1 hour.

3 Divide the mixture into 4 portions. Roll out each portion into a thin circle and cut each circle into quarters.

4 Heat the oil in a deep frying pan and fry the quarters until golden brown.

Note: *The mixture will puff up very quickly when fried. For variety, dust with icing sugar or add cinnamon to icing sugar and sprinkle on top. Serve hot.*

Coconut cookies

INGREDIENTS

1 cup of grated coconut

½ cup of sugar or icing sugar

1 cup of plain flour

1 teaspoon of baking powder

8 tablespoons of melted butter

PROCEDURE

1. Mix the coconut, sugar, flour and baking powder together.
2. Pour the melted butter over the ingredients and mix well.
3. Roll small pieces of the mixture into balls and place on a greased baking sheet. Flatten the balls.
4. Bake over a medium heat for about 20 minutes.

Goolgoolas (sweet)

INGREDIENTS

4 cups of self-raising flour

1 cup of sugar

1 teaspoon of crushed cardamom

cold water

oil for frying

PROCEDURE

1. Mix together the flour, sugar and cardamom.
2. Add enough cold water to make a thick batter.
3. Heat the oil in a frying pan.
4. Drop spoonfuls of batter into the oil and fry until golden brown.
5. Drain on a clean tea towel.

Note: *You can add sultanas or raisins for variety. These goolgoolas can be eaten hot or cold.*

Goolgoolas with banana (sweet)

INGREDIENTS

1 cup of mashed banana

¾ cup of sugar

3 cups of self-raising flour

1 teaspoon of nutmeg

cold water

oil for frying

PROCEDURE

1. Mix the banana, sugar, flour and nutmeg together.
2. Add enough cold water to make a thick, smooth batter.
3. Put aside for 10 minutes.
4. Heat the oil in a frying pan and fry spoonfuls of the mixture in the oil.

5. Drain on a clean tea towel.

 **Note:** *These goolgoolas can be eaten hot or cold.*

Foolowries (savoury)

INGREDIENTS

3 small onions or spring onions

1–2 chillies

4 cups of self-raising flour

1½ teaspoons of salt (to taste)

cold water

oil for frying

PROCEDURE

1. Finely slice or chop the onions.
2. Crush the chillies and add to the onions.
3. Add the flour and salt to this mixture, then add enough water to make a thick batter.
4. Heat the oil to a medium heat in a deep frying pan and drop spoonfuls of the batter into the oil.
5. Fry until golden brown.
6. Drain on a clean tea towel.

Note: *These foolowries can be eaten hot or cold.*

Yams

Yams have a high protein content. The yam often plays an important part in the traditional culture in Papua New Guinea.

The yam is a climbing vine. It forms starchy underground tubers that come in a wide variety of shapes and sizes. There is a lot of work associated with growing yams and they are expensive to buy.

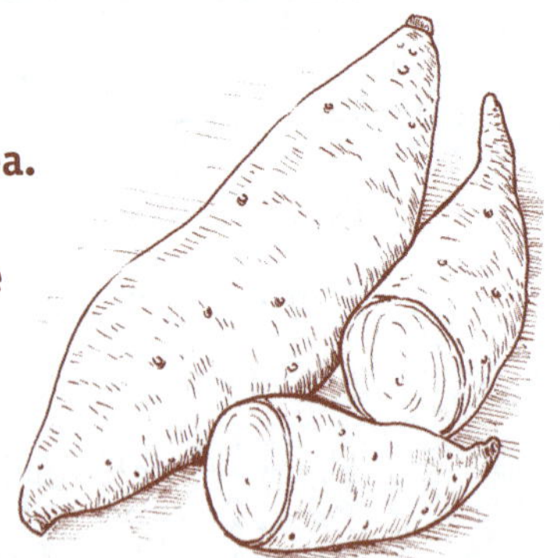

Yam curry with coconut cream

INGREDIENTS

1 medium-sized yam
1 clove of garlic
3 cups of warm water
1 curry leaf
salt to taste
1 onion
1 coconut
2 tablespoons of oil
½ teaspoon of curry powder

PROCEDURE

1 Peel the yam and cut into small squares. Wash the yam pieces.
2 Chop the onion and crush the garlic.
3 Scrape the coconut. Squeeze the coconut milk into 3 cups of warm water.
4 Heat the oil in a saucepan and add the curry leaf. (The leaf will split.)
5 Add the onion and garlic and fry until light in colour.
6 Add the yam pieces, curry powder and salt to taste. Stir well.
7 Add about 2 cups of water and cook with the lid on until the water has been absorbed.
8 Add the coconut cream and cook until the yams are soft. Stir occasionally.

Note: *This dish is very tasty. It can be served with rice or Indian bread (roti).*

Yam chips

INGREDIENTS

1 large yam
oil for frying
salt to taste

PROCEDURE

1 Peel the yam. Wash and dry well.
2 Slice the yam into 1 cm (½ inch) rounds, then cut across into fingers.
3 Heat the oil in a deep pan and fry the yam chips until golden brown. Drain well.
4 Sprinkle with salt before serving.

Yam fritters

INGREDIENTS

1 large yam
1 teaspoon of baking powder
1 chicken cube
2 cups of plain flour
salt to taste
oil for frying

PROCEDURE

1 Peel the yam, wash and dry it, and cut as for chips.
2 Mix the flour with the baking powder, salt and chicken cube. Add just enough water to make a smooth paste.
3 Heat enough oil for frying.
4 Drop the yam pieces in the batter, one handful at a time, and coat well.
5 Drop the battered yam pieces in the hot oil and fry until golden brown.
6 Drain well before serving.

Note: *Different spices can be added to the batter to make these fritters even tastier.*

Glossary

bake	cook food in an oven, or in an enclosed space where the heat is dry
beat	stir something briskly
boil	cook food in very hot bubbling water or other liquid
chop	cut food into small pieces
cream	mix ingredients until they have a creamy consistency
dice	cut food into small cubes
dissolve	mix something with a liquid so that it becomes part of the liquid
fold	gently mix one ingredient into another
fry	cook food in a pan with oil or fat
grate	shred food into small pieces
grease	rub oil or margarine onto a baking tray or tin so that the food will not stick when it is cooked
knead	mix dough with your hands by folding and turning until it becomes smooth
marinate	place food in a liquid mixture and let it stand for some time so that it absorbs the flavours
mash	crush a food such as potato or sweet potato until it is soft
mix	blend all ingredients until smooth
peel	remove the outer layer from a vegetable or fruit
sift	put flour or a similar substance through a sieve to remove any lumps
slice	cut food into thin flat pieces